Just Like

SIBLINGS

By
Blessed E Oki
And
Akin M Olaolu

8/16/02

Father, Accept the first fruit of our labour and let it be according to your will. Blessed for Akin & Blessed

I

Library of Congress Control Number: 2002093204

ISBN 0 – 9721336 – 0 - 7

First printing

Printed in the U.S.A by
Morris Publishing
3212 East Highway 30
Kearney, NE 68847
1-800-650-7888

JUST LIKE

SIBLINGS

A COLLECTION

OF

POEMS

AND

INSPIRATIONAL THOUGHTS

By

Blessed E Oki And Akin M Olaolu

We acknowledge the wisdom and grace given us by our heavenly father. We also thank him for this great opportunity that enables us to share with you some of life issues.

Just Like Siblings is the first volume of a collection of poems, prose, prayers and inspirational thoughts composed by Blessed Oki and Akin Olaolu

Both authors perception of God as father is magnified in this book as they rejoice in their heavenly and earthly heritage

This is a parent/child poetry book of poems, prose and inspirational thoughts dedicated to all the children of God, the righteous as well as the weak and feeble.

Our profound gratitude is to our friends
and editors Olutooke and Alphonso.

We appreciate the influence of all those that have been used by God to bless us and hereby extend our thanks to the entire staff of the Small Business Center of the city of Greater Durham, North Carolina including all their affiliates

PROLOGUE

Let us read to the health of the one

Who is wild, yes

Wildly at ease with life

Who never seeks solace

From winter in summer,

For summer, winter, spring and fall

Are all but seasons,

Times, in the bigger sphere of time.

Let us read to the health of the one

Who is Us but is not of Us

 Let us read to the health of the mind

TABLE OF CONTENTS

Joyous Bay

It is a glorious day
Recuperating on his joyous bay
Days ago I was disappointed
It was not his time appointed
Through this his love is revealed
To a child loved before conceived

Now dear Lord I pray
Lead this fear of mine to bay,
Your Help in ages past recall
That faith is a never ceasing ball
The core of your child's existence
Prevailing over all human insurgence

Genesis

God in the beginning
Earth for his glory did create
New for his children heritage;
Even though we betray father's trust, and
Sin the fruit of knowledge wrought
In mercy eternal love prevailed
Savior died and we are reconciled

Promise

Worried about our future
Desirous to obey the Lord
Committed all to the father
Dwelling under his shadow

While in a dream
Me thought lost is all
There you were to stay
A promise God has made

Met a friend at the mall
Said a dream she had
Of a surprised parade
Confirms the promise is sure

Preacher he also sent
You need to keep your promise
Then wept I in gratitude
For love that would not let me go

Woman Oh Woman

Woman oh woman
Let go of the anger and hatred.
God gave you a precious gift to nurture
This gift depend on you to thrive
Elevate and appreciate this special one
Oh why must you destroy this child?

This is not about you
Striking and paralyzing as lightning
Obliterating the path of life as snow blizzard
Sweeping and destroying as tornado
Devastating as hurricane

Stop oh please stop
Spend a moment without rage
And appreciate this precious life
Entrusted to your care,
It is a privilege to work
With the author of life

For there is none greater
In heaven and on earth
Than this child of yours;
And this is your greatest blessing
Woman oh woman, be wise

Tomorrow

Tomorrow oh tomorrow
Tomorrow is a day away
Tomorrow is the day
Tomorrow oh tomorrow
Tomorrow is the day of his fulfillment,
What a teacher you are
Teaching patience and hope
Encouraging tender surrender
To him who knows tomorrow today;
Wait I plead with you
While I strive to understand today
How to live for him this day
Then let tomorrow testify of his grace.

All Over Again

You do it all over again
Through you I have come to so much gain
You awaken me to an upward thrust
Makes me marvel at your trust.

Traveling on the high way
Through the valleys and subways,
Driving back and forth
Worn out for all it's worth

You prevailed over my job
Gathering all the bob,
This is your gift
For I feel your lift
You are Lord, doing it all over again

Grandma Ruth

Grandma Ruth was the wisest woman
The wisest woman that ever lived
Only child of a king
Raised by the best
Though without formal education
She taught herself to read
Cooperating with her husband
She read only God's holy words

Grandma Ruth's principles were
Do not squander money
Fashion is seasonal
Clothing and articles depreciate in value
From the moment they are purchased
When in a strait
Your property are devalued
To promote sale and obtain needed cash
Grandma Ruth was an accountant
Investor, economist and designer

Never let anyone know they can hurt you
As your emotional weakness is a subject
The adversary will prey on.
Do not let the enemy know you are dying
Rather, stand tall; lift your head up high
March and stride like the elephant;
Crumble later in your secret chamber
Grandma Ruth was also a psychologist
Sociologist and philosopher

Never throw away food
For in your neighborhood
There must be someone in dare need;
All who ignore others need
Preferring waste to assisting
Will always come to want
No matter how blessed
Grandma Ruth was a philanthropist
Prudent, loving and kind

"I have been young now am I old
I have never seen the righteous forsaken
Nor her seed begging bread"
Were words of encouragement
To her widowed daughter
For she knew of the Lord
That supplied all her needs
Since her provision never failed
Grandma Ruth daughter of faith
Full of trust in him that never fails

You have a short while to live
Life is like the grass
Full grown and blooming today,
Trimmed, cut and withered tomorrow;
You owe it to yourself
To serve your creator
While his breath is still in you
Grandma Ruth child of a king
Princess of the heavenly kingdom

Grandma Ruth was the wisest woman
The wisest woman that ever lived
For she found the secret
Of a happy life entwined in God:
The fear of the Lord was her wisdom
She committed her life to his service.
Three days before her death,
She prayed thus
"Lord now let thou thy servant
  Depart in peace according to thy word
  For mine eyes have seen thy salvation
  Which thou hast prepared
  Before the face of all people
  A light to lighten the Gentiles
  And the glory of thy people Israel"
Grandma Ruth greatest princess
Princess of the Almighty king.

Child Greatly Loved

When I consider your blessings
A sea that is never ebbing
It makes me marvel
That one used to gravel
Could receive so great a devotion
Beyond all human comprehension

Father to this child
Forgiving while gently he chides,
Prevails over all that falsely attracts
To ensure she stays on track;
She in constancy he reassures
Through a daily provision that is sure

Oh child greatly loved
Touched by his spirit as the dove
When will you the father trust
Who maintains your upward thrust?
From his presence do not deflect
Then his beauty you will reflect.

Let Go

Awarded scholarship for grades
Sent away to learn trades,
In view of disrupted academic excellence
Concealed rage festers in your existence

But let go, let go of the past
He knows you have been through a blast
God remembers all your pain
He has poured you showers of rain

For you were supplanted and repressed
Your offspring he planted and blessed
See the ever-flowing seas
Of blessings that never cease

He Laughs

Many a time he warned her
Using an unusual messenger
Be bold to have a child
This is your only chance.

When tortured to get rid of her son
Victory she gained through hymns sung

Left in pillory to raise this special gift
Strength she received by his lift

God have a spectacular sense of humor
Trust me and let go of this humbugger
Do it; forgiveness is graceful
The Lord laughs, as she is grateful

The Lord's Supervision

He despised her for not yielding
Excluding her from his teachings
Thought spite a great weapon
An innocent child to spun

It was obvious to all as toggery
His kindred were in constant quandary
Why does he hate this child so much?
None could ever suspect the root of such

He empowered her with the wisdom
That preserves her freedom
Prevailing over all human suppression
She thrives on the Lord's supervision

Africa Oh Africa

Africa oh Africa
Land richly blessed
Center of the world
The sun rises from your shore
To embrace the world at large
What happened to your children?
Often squabbling and fighting
They have forgotten your teaching
Of the unity in a bunch of broomsticks;
This was grandfather's last bequest
To his children on his deathbed,
For it's not easy said he
To break the bunched broomsticks
But once separated,
Each can be broken and destroyed

Africa oh Africa
Your children squabble and fight
'Your fathers sold us as slaves'
Where is their long-term memory?
Homeland had to plead and
Many a times fought for independence.
Your greatest joy is your children
Through treachery and subtlety
Were they stolen from you
Oh how your heart longed and ached
For children separated from your bosom

11

Africa oh Africa
Your children squabble and fight
When will they cease from anger?
They all believe in God
But fail to appreciate his providence
That the Lord has sent them
To preserve a multitude of people;
Ignorantly their hearts and minds are shut
To this great provision of the Lord
Depriving themselves of joy and praise
They thrive on hurt and spite

Africa oh Africa
Your children squabble and fight.
Now dear Lord I pray,
Reach out to Africa's children
That they may embrace the wisdom
In the unity of the bunched broomsticks;
United they maintain a clean environment
And none can break or bend them.
Let Africa heave a sigh of relief
As her children unite in joy and praise
All squabbling and fighting ceased

Africa oh Africa
Your children have arrived at shore
Into a haven of peace
With a perfect understanding that
Our steps are ordained

To touch every shore God has made
For we are the apple of his eye

Grace That Never Shrinks

Lord here comes my kindred
Who are your children
They are so full of righteousness
Without room for gracious forgiveness

Children who are so well
Can afford on self to dwell
While walking with up turn nose
Saving grace they may not know

Great physician of the sick
Grant unto those who seek
Complete pardon from sin
Grace that never shrinks

In The Image Of God

Black is the color of my hair
My skin is of a different blend
With age my hair turns silver
But none can tell the color of my skin

The blackboard is black
I write with the white chalk
Never met a white or black man
For none of such exist

The color spectrum cannot inculcate me
It is a figment of human imagery
But it behooves me to comprehend
That some are white and others black

One day we will understand
That skin color is not in the spectrum,
We are fearfully and wonderfully made
In the image of God

We are the image of God
Hence there is no color to the skin.
Thank God for making us in his image
Of the color that befits his glory

Immensely Blessed

Here I am Lord
A heart filled with gratitude
For all your benefits,
It has not entered into human imagination
How much you love me.

You move in all mysterious ways
Calming my stress, you continually say
'It is I be not afraid'.
Can sinner such as I
Be immensely blessed?

It's real; you walk and talk with me
Reveal the future too
Oh grace, grace
What can I do without you?

Accented Freedom

Freedom, what freedom?
It is a case of mistaken identity.
My tonation may differ
And talking fast my lot
Why not hear me out?
You prefer to tune off

With an outrageous indignation
She does not belong here.
I comprehend you because I listen
If I pretend not to understand
You tell me I am stupid
And if my speech is slow,
You assume native language translation.
My voice is a gift from God
Freedom allows me to be myself.
In fear of embarrassment,
This one refuses to communicate
You rustle round for interpreter
It is his right to be understood,
Is this freedom a sham?
It is obvious to all
That you are partial and judgmental
Whatever is good for the goose
Is not good for the gander
Inequality is paramount.
It is amazing that
A society with altered tonation
And variation of English dialects,
Differing in speech and accents
By the span of hair strands
Castrates one and builds the other;
Lord see man's injustice to man
Freedom, what freedom?

Thank You

I've never met you before
Yet you hate me passionately
These were your words to me
'I don't want you to touch that
Who do you think you are?
You and your crazy accent'
Interjectionally I smiled, look
This is the voice God gave me
No one can change it.
You are more infuriated
'You come into this room
Thinking you are some kind of a goddess
Let me tell you, you are a-nobody
You walk in with your nose in the air
As if you've got no problem
Why don't you fix your problem first,
Before trying to help someone else?
Get out just get out
I don't want you to come back'
Thank you for being so mean
It motivated me to reach out
God's gift and provision to accept
Thank you for being an instrument
Used to compel this child
The father's promise to receive
Thank you for being in my life that day

For while you were raving and cursing
A silent voice I heard saying
Arise, enter into the joy of the Lord thy God.
Thank you, oh thank you enormously
May the Lord richly bless you,
For being in my life that day
I just want to thank you.

Long Days In The Land

Honor your parents is a law,
It blooms with the injunction
That your days may be long
In the land that God has given you.
What a blessed promise
That flows out of honor
Never yourself these blessings deny,
Honor to the good and evil
The evil abandon, neglect and abuse
Depriving themselves of the greatest gift,
But you child deserves better
Let no man steal your joy
Nor deprive you of your promised days.
Love the good forgive the evil
Give thanks for your situation
Do not punish yourself
Or rob yourself of long days
In the land given by the Lord thy God

Gored Into Action
Then Ambushed

The people were gored into action
They knew their freedom was at stake
Hence they voted en masse for him.
He led the votes said the media
This irate others
Then was a strange victory announced,
The people have been ambushed
Their freedom stolen by subtleness;
How did this happen?
This nation pride herself on freedom,
Where is justice?
Her foundation of choice is being rocked.
It's a shame real shame
That a fraction of supposed investors
Are holding the nation to ransom.
Perhaps you have forgotten,
God rules in the affairs of men
He alone knows the truth.
If this is an injustice from the people
To the people by the people,
Our God in his mercy
Will cut off the impostors
And uphold his grace.
Let us all therefore
Lift our eyes unto the hill
Where our help abounds

One Nation

Oh my Lord!
No one will ever be sure
Each accusing the other
Nothing short of a miracle
Allows the people's wish to triumph.
Thought justice and truth are
Indelible marks on the laws of the land
Offering all the people choice to respect
Necessitating no legal rambling.
Unfortunately, the law is being wangled
Nauseating are the finger pointing
Doubtless the people are weary
Emergent are distraught children
Rambling role models observing;
Gone are the devoted leaders
Opulent in wisdom and gracious
Devoted to service led by God

Affirmative Action

Almighty father
Foreigners do direct
Forming this nation
Indignant are some
Race is the issue
Manifested by skin color
African Americans they are called
Though born here, hence citizen
Indirect discrimination
Vested by government
Encouraged through data base
Affirmed in quota system.
Can we do away with color and
Treat all citizens as one?
Injustice of man
Overtly portrayed as concern
Notional to freedom

Almighty father continually brings
Folks to inhabit this land
From the four corners of this world
Irrespective of tongue or color
Requiring that they love all
Modeling the Lord's household
Acceptance of this truth
Transforms all human societies

Into the original design
Versatile in peaceful coexistence
Energizing to great heights,
Affording a solid foundation
Cultivated in respect to all and for all.
Time and season will not
Infringe on or alter the blessings
Of a people that treasure life
Nurtured by the designer alone

Almighty father
Forgive them for this error
Forging on discrimination
Involving dual standard
Reticent on color and race
Mandate no color or race database
All Americans treated as one,
Time will denote
Intelligence is an equal opportunity
Vehemently sort and attainable,
Emergent in the freedom
Available for all to strive and thrive;
Culture of segregation is abolished
Triumph on affirmative action established
Irrespective of color, creed and speech
Opportune all to excel
Now Lord help us this to comprehend

Glory In Honor

Got a flight for 237
Days ago it was 397
Your teaching on caring my focus,
'Whatever you may profit by me
Is given to the Lord'
Bless your parents with your substance
Rather than world's acknowledgement,
Let your words always be my guide

My Brother

Spending time lately to recollect
A wonderful childhood with you
Who taught me to appreciate music
Blessed assurance Jesus is mine a favorite;
You also taught me to read, run and trust
Remember you woke up Easter morning
And the Lord Jesus you claimed to have seen
We spent that Easter gazing up
If only to catch a glimpse of Christ;
I have spent a lot of time recently
Just thanking God for you.
It thrills me to learn of your leadership
As in your quiet loving way,
You are caring for the family
You have a perfect understanding

Of the legacy of Ruth and Jacob;
With you as my brother
I've learnt to carry myself with dignity
You are the epitome of grace.

Heritage Of The Living God

We are the heritage of the living God
He is our strength and stay,
King Itade's throne was usurp
When sent away from home
Subsequent to his father's death,
His uncle reigned for a while
But God in his mercy intervened
Motivating the women in the town,
His purpose for Itade he fulfilled.
Princess Ruth his only child
Is a living testimony of our family
God we honor through choice,
He fights all our battles
He maintains our course
He ensures we stand in his promise.
Itade did attain the throne promised
To him from the world's foundation,
This is your heritage child
Heritage established by the Lord

Flight 237

Deferred flight after this occasion
What a glorious decision
The world's praise to forfeit
Parents' care is the profit
Then was her world enlarged,
Flight reduced by a third at large
Oh what a joyous reward
From him who keeps his word,
You prove yourself faithful
Over and over again

Created For This Cause

When I consider your goodness
The beauty of your coolness
Father of unconditional love
Bears me on the wings of the dove
Always making for me a way
Your name to glorify everyday

You reduced every cost
That I may not be lost
To me you sent help
That faith might have depth

Before me you preceded
That grace to me be added

In your presence may I continually dwell
My praise to you forever swells
None will separate me from your course
For you created me for this cause
As you are my light
Let me in you delight

Let The People Be

Dear creator, help your people
Who are being treated as puppets
Your original design is being altered
For none is allowed to be.
An active and inquisitive child
With eagerness and extreme energy does search
Ready to absorb all your wondrous works
Is labeled with attention deficit disorder.
The quiet and introverted
That thinks about these things
In order to praise your name
Is said to suffer from depression,
Those that fear standing out in the crowd
Are managed for social anxiety disorder.
Please help, potter of these clay
Intervene on behalf of your creatures
Who are being altered
Let your design be seen unaltered

God Sent Help

He was poor and desolate
His body ravaged and diseased
He was man's despot,
His providers were nonchalant
Sporadic were the treatments.
Then lift up caregivers prayers
Lord this could be me if not for grace
Oh God you sent help
The state did intervene
A dream the social worker confirmed
For he was made new

Grace For Every Moment

What a glorious day
Driving here is a pleasure
Workload beyond imagination
And the folks are friendly
Giving me continuous incentive
To glorify him that keeps me,
Providing grace for every moment
Oh how blissful it is to trust you
Grant that my slippery steps
Be planted in you
And none from your love can sever

Black Ice

Black ice she is famed
Lord see how she feigned
Accusation for unfounded flounder;
Conspiratorial and slick in nature
Kindling a wild range of fire
Inconsequential of the irksomeness,
Compounding series of allegations
Encountered when sort for clarification

Bulwark ever so strong
Lord towers above the wrung of
Activities beyond human concept
Counsels, guides and precepts
Knocking down the wall of my mocker,
Irrevocable praise to my maker
Comforts me in every situation
Elevating above attempted humiliation

Black ice she is called
Lord interceded and charged
Angels to bear the car and I,
Crash prevented in a slither by his care
Knowledge of which is awesome.
Immortal love of the father
Comprehended through this gesture
Expands this child's candor

Counting The Drive

Toying with the ambu bag
Not counting the breaths drag
She stopped her with a dagger
How many breaths did you give?
Really she was not counting the drive,
His countenance a mock delight
Justified his flunked test in light,
Lord why does he contend with her?
His follies in this please suspend

The Potter's Eyesight

Lord she came in weary
Contemplating withdrawing,
Remembering to listen to your message
Which are your words through all ages
Listen but don't do what they do
Keep your eyes on the potter
While he shapes and mould you,
Grace she perceived
Through the potter's eyesight
Oh blessed Savior
Nothing shall separate her from you

Mirror Image

While in the shower
The image of God she contemplates,
Lord you are my mirror
Wish I were a perfect reflection
The mirror image of heavenly father,
Guiding in every situation
Redeeming the weary
Accepting the prodigal
Counseling the lost
Embracing the lonely
Forgiving all his children
Unshackling those in bondage
Upholding the righteous
Loving unconditionally
What a graceful mirror

Lord I Have A Home

Offspring of freedom
Imbued with boldness and wisdom
Princess of the heavenly kingdom
Lord I have a home

The House

Your word is so bight
It is my only source of light
Love to worship in your house
Where your people are roused
While at the throne
Wishing for a home
Praying with hope
Help came on a hop,
You sent guidance
Directions flowed in abundance
Lord let this place be
A place of grace and beauty

Life Issues

Its me Lord, standing on your hallway
Reaching out to your hem on the pathway
This touch that stops life issues
Enclose me with mercy, for you paid the dues
After the agonizing night of mourning
You give joy in the morning,
Let me your rod with comfort beat
Your prevailing prayer prevents my shifting as wheat
While with me you are wrestling
I cling to you for your blessing

Oh Lord She Wails

Created in beauty
To do God's duty
She yielded her loyalty
To the unworthy of humanity

Endowed with perfect heart of love
The apple of the eye of God above
She her master betrays
While after man she strays

Oh Lord! She wails
Why me all these bewails?
As her heart in humiliation bows,
She is touched by his rainbow

With A Kiss

Judas did him with a kiss betray
This I contemplate and I am afraid
For Him with a kiss we do betray
While after Man we trail
Sin is like the dope
God is our only hope

Delightsome Land Holy Sacred

Down on our knees
Even as they mock and jeer
Lord please walk with us
In every step we take
Grant us the opportunity
Heaven's grace to share
Testifying of our father's love
Stronger than all the darts of tongues
Often wagging and destructive
Mutilating the weak and feeble.
Eternal father of grace
Let your weak and feeble
Accept your favor and rise
Nurture us for your glory alone to
Dwell under your wings,
Happy for your kind understanding
Opportune to worship at your feet
Let us live with the blessed assurance that
You have purchased us for your praise.
Sanctify and reconcile us
According to your manifold blessings,
Consecrate us for your worship and
Redeem us for heaven above
Eternal father may we for ever be
Devoted to you alone

Daddy Son To
Father Above

How his heart aches
To make everything perfect
That his children may be without defect

Then came an earthquake
Which established his love
With the children that he adores

God also aches
When his children detects
Things he made that we he may protect

God sends us the quakes
In order to look above and appreciate
Love on the wings of a dove

What height of joy awaits
This daddy, son to father above
Who clings to unfailing love

Now With Joy

Daddy oh daddy
How I wish things were different
Thought you didn't care
Your little child abandoning

Now with joy I appreciate
This wonderful name you gave me
That the blessings of God
Will continually be with me

Thank you for being so thoughtful
You did it out of love
I am truly blessed
The Lord dwells with me

Your prayer for my future
Before I was conceived in the womb
Is magnified and enlarged
Through the grace of him
In whose care you committed me

Heal All Hurts

He was only a child
When his world crashed
Now in his first year of manhood
His zeal for achievement is in a hood.

Lord in his grief and hurt
He is willing his future to halt
One of the most brilliant
Endowed and gifted as none but deviant
He sits back as life slips by
Time also fleets while he sleeps

Grant him oh Lord we pray
With his future not to play
Except you rise and help
He will self destroy in his steps

Unto you that heal all hurts
We lift him up that he may not halt
The beautiful life you have ordained
Let him arise reach out and obtain
Understanding, wisdom, joy and peace
While you mold and mend his life pieces

Wonderful Friend

What a wonderful friend
Whose loyalty never ends,
You have been with us
Through all the toss
Bruised but not scarred
Frightened yet not scared

Weeping nights yet we sing
Through fire and not singed
We are weary but not tired
Discouraged not in despair
Deserted but not destitute
Elected children not substitutes

You continue to elevate
That we might be brave
As to you our voices we raise
Your holy name we praise
And in you we boast
Who is the king of host

Renew Thy Spirit

Righteous and Holy Father
Eternal grace dwells with you
Nothing is too hard for you
Even as you listen to this child
When her world was in tumult
Triumphantly you lifted her up
Heaven rejoice at your tender mercy
You are worthy to be praised.
She for a while slipped from your spirit
Pressure of life weighing her down
In love you reconciled her to yourself.
Renew thy spirit within her
Imbue her with your loving kindness
Take away self give carefree confidence
Which imbues her to trust your judgement
In all her life your guidance she sees
Taking her to heights unknown
Hedging her into an impenetrable shelter
In which no harm can touch her.
Now as in your name she glory
Make her to always remember
Extraordinary abiding bliss in your tower

Sacred Promise

What a great man of valor
Raised with dignity and honor
But he was the son of a harlot
Begotten of a strange woman,
Rejected and deprived by his lot
He fled from the presence of man.
They turned to him in their distress
Pleading with the detected to bear the rule,
Mistrust and abuse were all he witnessed
But recalled victory when God is the ruler.
With the enemy he did boast
Of the Lord's heritage and possession
Which was a gift from the Lord of hosts
Who won the victory in our progression
Accustomed to being used and discarded,
He promised him that never fails
A sacrifice of first contact if victory is accorded
As his vision was in a veil.
Triumphant his steps home bounded
Out came his girl with timbres and dances
Good grief his only love is branded.
Though lowly esteemed
Both in this instance knew him that bears them
He that bears on the wings of the dove
For he lost his only joy it seem
When he surrender the one that he loved

The people that deride him to redeem,
What is your vow today?
What did you promise the omniscience?
Pay your promised vow without blemish
For he whom you have promised is faithful
Since he can count on your loyalty
He makes your efforts dainty and joyful
As he enriches and rewards royally

Glorious Day

Lord what a glorious day
You make me joyous and gay
Pulling me out of the dread
Along life's narrow pathway I tread

This is the crossroad of life
The intersection where faith is alive
Doubt and self here abates
When in you I maintain my gait

Even though there be a dearth
And the world be a hearth,
In you I have peace
For you fix my life pieces

Eat Not, Touch Not,
Die Not

There is a forbidden fruit for each man
With a decisive choice for death or life
For Eve it was knowledge and desire
For Adam it was compassion and finger pointing
For Abel it was God's acceptance and brotherly betrayal
For Cain it was jealousy and anger
For Noah it was courage in the unseen
For Abraham it was fear, denial and surrender
For Sarah it was love and submission
For Isaac it was contentment and favoritism
For Rebecca it was prediction and partiality
For Esau it was rashness and carelessness
For Jacob it was subtlety and aspiration
For Leah it was rejection and a complex
For Rachel it was an idol and deceit
For Dinah it was loneliness, wandering and rape
For Judah it was succession and a pledge
For Tamar it was frustration and harlotry
For Joseph it was separation and guidance
For Moses it was relinquish of power and true God
For Deborah it was leadership and communication
For Samson it was sex and vexation
For Gideon it was trust and victory
For Ruth it was God and family

41

For Hannah it was provocation and perplexity
For Samuel it was devotion and purity
For Eli it was priesthood and parenthood
For Saul it was obedience and justification
For David it was covetousness and responsibility
For Nabal it was drunkenness and hospitality
For Abigail it was intercession and forbearance
For Absalom it was forgiveness and vengeance
For Solomon it was innocence and wisdom
For Elijah it was true worship and a fiery chariot
For the Shunamite it was generosity and a child
For Esther it was position and deliverance
For Job it was faithfulness and friends
For Daniel it was prayer and persecution
For Mishael it was fire and presence of the Almighty
For Jonah it was fear of mockery and whale sail
For Ezra it was the adversary and building of God's house
For Elizabeth it was encouraging cooperation
For Mary it was ridicule and joy to the world
For Peter it was loyalty and repentance
For Judas it was a kiss and suicide
For Paul it was over zealousness and transformation
For Dorcas it was wealth, caring and sharing
For Jesus it was the ultimate sacrifice for our redemption
What is your forbidden fruit?
Watch therefore and learn
Eat not touch not die not

Knowledge Of Good
And Evil

Allowed to eat of every tree freely
Except from the tree that is deadly
Then comes the subtle creature
That knows about falling nature
Questioning a separated one in retrospect
For she desired wisdom as an aspect
Of the fruit good for food and pleasant
As her eyes behold it this instance.
This fruit she did eat
And gave her husband of it
The result was nakedness and shame,
Garments of figs as apron their aim
A covering from the face
Of him who is full of grace;
He walks in the cool of the day
To visit with his children and play,
Today they are in hiding
From the author of good tidings;
Neither accepted responsibility
Finger pointing for accountability
Then was the ground cursed with thistles
While she became subordinate and brittle
Bringing forth in sorrow and pain
The death row was the gain.
The creature lost its dignified estate

Its deceptive actions led to this state.
You have a garden planted
But the forbidden fruit is painted
By him that wants you supplanted
With knowledge he will have you tainted.
God trust you and bought you at a price
Let not the knowledge of good and evil entice

Forbidden Fruit

Forbidden to eat of this fruit
Openly situated at the center
Requiring obedience and trust
But she desired knowledge and wisdom
Implied by the deceiver
Deadly is the repercussion of eating
Destruction follows disobedience
Evil and good are the knowledge gained
None will live after eating
Fruit of knowledge so lethal
Root of all evils yet unseen
Unique and perpetual to all children
Initiated into the agony of disobedience
Trust and grace alone paid the price

Loving Father

What a wonderful restless child
And father will not chide
Knowing the evil of the world,
He reasoned with him in his word
Do not waste your life he pleaded
But oh boy! He was decided
Pleasure and delight were all in his note
Awaiting him was life without a father who dotes

Friends flowed by the litter
While his life glittered
Then time cut him short
The downward trend to halt
Father's loving care he recollects
From mercy he did not recoil
He ceased his labor lost of a deviant
Aware of tender care of father's servants

Lord I have wasted so much time
Time nudged him as moments chime
His pride he did swallow
His loving father to hallow
Father spotted his son in distraught
Then ran to meet him with his trust
As toward home he trod
In warm embrace he was hugged

Many have refused to blink
For it is others fault they think,
Failing to seek him in their plight
As pride blinds their eyesight;

This father and son had a relationship
The world's lust was a temporary worship
Trust compelled him toward home to turn
In love and joy father watched his return.
Before you leave this shelter
Establish a relationship with his altar
In hours of need you will recall
His tender mercy and not recoil

In The Long John

Let Johnny stay in the long john
For this missy will not miss him
Since the promise of roses
Cannot be compared to the care
Of him that gave Johnny to John
Who also gave John to missy,
So Johnny's stay in the long john
Will not deprive missy of John.
As long as Johnny stays in the long john
The promise to missy
Of John with Johnny in the long john
Is fulfilled in full
This is the secret of abstinence

Weary But Not Discouraged

Walk with him that never faints
Even as life billows roll
Acknowledge him that is not weary
Running the affairs of his creatures
Your walking and running he observes,
Bearing you up with strength
Upon wings as the eagle
Teaching you to observe all things,
Nothing can harm you in his shelter
Only keep your eyes on him
Then the darts of distraction
Definitely shall not prevail.
Immersed in his love and care
Strength you receive anew,
Climb every mountain with him
Or into the valley with him descend.
Unshackled by his grace alone
Rise in his glory to heights unknown,
Acquitted by heaven at last
Gone are the binding fetters
Eternal peace is here to stay
Dwelling in the presence of the Almighty

None Can Understand

None can understand this love
Embracing me as the dove
Innocent and pure with delight
Teaching me joy as the dawn of light

He bears me up in his arms
Ever protecting me from harm
Renewing within me his strength
With peace of life at length

Eagle's wings his gift amounts
Allowing me to rise and mount
Running I am not weary
You may wonder at our story

Now I walk and do not faint
On this path his hand paints
Ruminating on his word every step I take
For in his love I bathe

As he leads me incessantly
In him I glory eternally
Now with you this love I share
He is neither weary nor faint in his care

Times And Seasons

Let me not walk behind you
As your plans I will delay
Nor run and walk ahead of you
For my walk would be in vain
Grant me the grace to walk with you,
My life in harmony with yours
And the times and seasons
Would testify of your glorious guidance

Let me not tarry
When you want me to go forth
Nor march and run
When you want me to be still
Rather, keep me in tune with you
That your purposes for my life
Might be fulfilled
In your time

Silent Ruler

She is quiet and unassuming
Submissive trusting and loving
Reveling in him who her heart revere,
Condescending wise and bold
You consider her none assertive
Yet she rules his kingdom,
For he knows her consistency
He understands her salient wisdom
But she is often unheard of
Allowing him to take the praise.
Wherefore he adores her,
Who is his inscrutable mastermind
Propelling him to opulence with hortatory
Since she is earth's motivator
The silent voice that rules the world

Greatest Force Of Nature

Water, you are a great essential of life
You were born before earth's foundation
From you all things borrow life
And none survives without you,
But your fury none can stand

Air is your sister and she is free
Filled with elements that life thrives on

She breezes by and blows in our homes
A welcome companion of our lives,
But she rages and sweeps all in her path

Your sister Sunlight is warm and friendly
She cheers our hearts and sights
With her we neither fumble nor grope
She hides and we stumble or starve
Boy! We are toast in her anger

Dews and mist are your babies
Along with sun and air, they nurture all creation
When you all are united.
Rain falls, lightning flashes, thunder roars
All for our benefit and blessing
The rainbow reassures of life continuity

Oh what a terrible disaster
When these three contend
Striving for mastery over earth
Water stretches and sweeps in hurricane
Air whirls, grasps and sucks in tornado
Light hides and obliterate our paths in blizzard
Sparking roaring fire in thunderstorm.

None of these compares with her
That is the greatest force of nature
Since she wrest the earth from God
Earth is reconciled with heaven through Christ

Happy Birth Day

Happy birth day Mama
This is your birth day
For on the day you gave birth
All heaven and earth rejoiced
In unison the echo rang
It's a boy

This is your first boy child
A source of so much joy
Nurtured in the fear of God
He is full grown and blessed
He is your son

It seems he is departed
From the knowledge you impacted
The world embracing
While from God he is racing
He is a man

Simply hold on Mama
Your words are like manna
He will never forget
As on life journey he forges
He is your loyal son

With the host of heaven now rejoice
As he unites with heaven in his choice
Returning to love that will not let him go
For his peace is your goal
Mama your son is back

The Lord's Puzzle

He is a gift from the Lord
For treasure and love
He perceives himself as a trophy
For conquer and display
Seeking only those that captures
Overlooking the one that raptures

Rejecting the Lord's puzzle
Preferring things that dazzle
Constantly turning to the glitters
Pulling away from God's shelter
Open now his eyes
Less his heart be iced

Father help him to be humble
That from you he does not tumble
Climb with him this hill
And incline him to your will
Grant him your grace
As in love your name he praise

This Shore

Here we are on this shore
And each of us must set sail
Only by his grace do we prevail
Over inner and outer turbulence of war

The water around us surge
As we strive to conquer the storm
Ranging within and without the stern
That fills the cistern of life urges

One thing is common to all
For we all desire to worship
The one that is great in stock
Of manifold blessings in his Lordship

Some by virtue of the greatest miracle
Are able to accept his attributes
While others debate and compare articles
Spending life away from him in solitude

But none can afford to stay idle
For the rudder we must handle
Is the decisive force of the radar
That propels us to sail on this water

Deliverance

This is another birthday
Better than all other days
For God gave her a gift
Similar to the time
She was from the womb lifted,
For she never had the opportunity
And the slightest cause for spontaneity
To recollect that first joyful cry
Which echo back to heaven
On her arrival at the haven
Of earth's wild shore
For life have rocked her sore.
But she was offered the incentive
That moved her to be attentive
As she called back to heaven
With overwhelming cry
On this her birthday
It was a reunion day.
She ceased after man to moan
Yielding herself to him that never roam
Forsaking everything that is inconsiderate
She clung to him that is compassionate
Standing up to life with a cry of joy
For this is the day of her deliverance
Restoring her remembrance
Of the might of the omnipotent
Her constant guide, friend and portion

The Toast

Let us read to the health of the one
Who is wild, yes
Wildly at ease with life
Who never seeks solace
From winter in summer;
For summer, winter, spring and fall
Are all but seasons,
Times, in a bigger sphere of time.
Let us read to the health of the one
Who is Us but is not of Us
Let us read to the health of the mind

Just Another Day

Just another day
Just another tomorrow come true
Another today gone by
Another yesterday created
Just another day closer to
Or farther from my dream
Truth is I don't know where I am
I don't know in what direction
I take this step
Don't know what today is today

Just another day
Just another tomorrow come through
Another today gone by
Just another peep
At what yesterday tomorrow turns out to be
The truth is I don't know .
If today is what yesterday promised
That tomorrow will be
But I do know
That God has not changed

It's A Miracle

To write down all my sorrows
Would be impossible
That life has being unfair to me
Would be an understatement
The bitterest of trials has
By some strange twist of fate beset me
It's not that I believe in fate
But it is in the face of grief
That I find it imperative to cry thus

It's a miracle that
I have strength today to hold this pen
For my heart ache above all things
My heart is lost at sea and fast drowning,

Oh! God has given me this strength
In him I shall trust still
He shall not fail me,
Surely he shall not

I Will Be There

If ever you grow weary
And you feel like giving up
If ever your knees go weak
And you feel like sitting down
Or you feel life have lost its purpose
Don't you give up
Don't you give up on me

Stand still and you will perceive
That I am with you and will always be
I will be the sun that brightens your day
The summer breeze that soothe you
The bower that shades you from storm

Whenever the rain cease not
Whenever it's chilly out there
Whenever the wind pierces through
Whenever life lacks meaning
Whenever the sky is all gray
Don't you dare give up
Don't you dare give up on me

As surely as the sun rises from east
As surely as the stars shine through the cloud
I will surely be with you
Even when your breath is ebbing away
I will surely be there for you

Thy Mercy In Rhyme

Oh how joy fills my soul
When thy mercy make manifest in me
Words whose meanings and rhyme
Fill my heart with wonder
It is amazing the power
That overflows my soul
When pretty faces with love
Open their mouths, their mouths in ardor
And thy praise utter with candor

So in as much as this mortal flesh
Shall from you breath lend,
And my lips, oh my lips
Shall find it possible to offer a word
Thus shall I allow thy mercy
To make manifest in me
Words whose meanings and rhyme
Fill human hearts with wonder

Thanks Buddy

When it was time
He knew it all
I don't know how he knew it
He just said it all,
I thought friendship was so complex
But you said it all
Thanks pal
Thanks buddy for being there

It was more than
What he said
It was more than his being there,
It was in knowing
That he was here
When I needed someone,
You're a pal buddy
It's about time you know that
Thanks buddy for being there

Wish I could do better
Than write this one for you
Wish I could mix yesterday
In retrospect and get it right,
But God knows why
God has plan for everyone,
For without you in my life

Who would have known
What a good friend is?
Thanks buddy for being there

Freedom To Worship

Weighed down and in the face of opposition
My soul slack as it was
Chose to on the fence of decision remain,
Ignorance and self-deceit indeed
Taught me to think the wall a palace of solace
Alas! It was only a wall,
And even on the wall I must choose a side
Which my complacent face shall face,
My soul no longer nonchalant
Chose to face the other side.

Since the good Lord could not
Watch me do me wrong,
So he did his wind blow
As I sought to turn away from him
He caused me to stumble from the wall.
I shall not therefore for I cannot
Lay claim to choosing the right side
Though prisoner I be on earth
Freedom is now mine
I will continually glory in his name
For my freedom to worship has just begun

Simple

How come they doubt you
When you are always around
Now I understand
For I too have fallen,
You are so simple
That the most simple
Comprehend you not

But you are all around,
A look at the stars
In their vast array
The beauty of these tell
That you are all around
Fruits that come in due season
With sweet delicacies tell
That you are all around

Simple we may be
Yet in the most complex
We seek comfort and rest
Observe experiment and test
That's what science has done
But we fail to try it on you
That is how simple the answer

Behold True Love

Some proud mother not too long ago
Looked at the stars and
She was with pleasure afflicted
For she saw the stars
Proudly hold up her son's image

Some proud son not too long after
Looked up at what man
Ignorantly calls space
And he saw love
And his eyes blurred with tears

Some creator being not too long after
(For time did not matter to him)
Sighed to an angel and said
"Behold thee true love,
  It was his mother's love
  That put his image in the star
  It was her son's love
  That did her a goddess make"

Ant Without A Company

I am like an ant without a company
Lost from the midst of friends
In the vast jungle of grasses
Situated quite a long way
Under yet another jungle of huge
Menacingly horrifying yet beautiful trees,
I am blind as the bat
Lost like a needle in a hay-sack.
The one thing I happen to know
Perhaps because it's a need to know situation
Is that "I am lost"
(But that should be apparent anyway)

There is no shelter for me
Others of my kind accept me not
For they are as blind as I
And scared of what they do not know,
Others still whose dubious company
Fate has granted me the pleasure
Of sharing this gloomy 'shelter' with
Are pricked with joy
Over one more lonesome wanderer
Whom they wholeheartedly wish to
On a first come-first serve basis devour as desert.
The one thing I happen to know
Perhaps because it's a need to know situation

Is that "I am butcher"
(But that should be apparent right?)

I am near loosing it
Near to loosing my mind
I have no idea of where I started out
No idea of where I am going
Blindly I grope for something to hold on to,
A little ray of light
A rough haggard path
Perhaps a path, which some part of me craves
A path traveled by one
Who in the palms of his hands my future holds.
The one thing that I happen to be sure of
Perhaps because it's a need to know situation
Is that "I am found"
(Now that is not apparent)

My Mum

I love you for the scolding
You never failed to give me
I love you for the nine months
You carried me within you
I love you for all the kisses and hugs
You have given me since the day I was born
I love you best not just
For being the best Mum on earth
But because you are my Mum

My Long Lost Friend

My long lost friend
He that my heart longs for
As we like the wheel of time
Roll our separate ways,
The words of our hearts
And the companionship of our souls
Festered in the maddest of times
For never is comfort from you ever far

My long lost friend
The memory of you in my heart
The finest poetry belies,
But how else shall I speak
Of the love of the one who is my all.
Flattery be not a gift to me
But if it be good to offer thee praise
I shall for thy sake forever thy goodness seek
Immortality derives its grandeur from you
For never is comfort from you ever far

Cry Aloud

Cry aloud my child
For your voice dear
Is heard amidst the crowd
For shame and pain
Shall no longer trap your veins
As with joy you lift your voice

Cry and make yourself be known
Disillusionment and confusion
Shall no longer becloud your vision
For the tears that hide the light from your face
Is gone with the pain.

How then shall you say?
"I see not him whose vision is my mirror"
How shall you not let
Not let your heart be known
As concerns so noble a task
How shall you not?

Best Of Friends

Last night I wept
As I remember the love that we shared
And how we used to live as one
Even as the very best of friends.
I was a fool to think
That without you
I could make it through the rain
Now I realize that without you
I am nothing

Knowing what I now know
Knowing that I am weak
And feeble without you beside me
Keeps me awake
I just can't sleep anymore
Though I try to keep these thoughts
These awful thoughts out of my head
Yet I know deep within me
I ought to ask for your forgiveness

So dear Jesus here I am
I've done this a lot of times before
I am sorry please forgive me
This is sincerely from the bottom of my heart
Please don't forsake me
You are my best friend

You Are Everything

As the trees sways gracefully
When the gentle summer wind blows
So are you when you walk,
Your strides are traced
With the grace and elegance
Of sunlight after a bleak thunderstorm
Yes, I am talking about you
Who says black ain't beautiful?
The blend of gray and black in your hair
Only God could have mixed
And your soft smooth skin
Only God could have molded.
What else can be that you ain't yet?

My goodness! It's not just silk but
Everything that you wear that glitters
The dancing stars in your eyes
Are like beams from a fair planet
I wish they would burn right through me.
What can a man want,
That you ain't already?
What can a woman wish she was,
That you ain't already?
You are everything there is
And everything there can be
Girl you are everything
That I have ever hoped for

There Are Times

There are times
When I turn my gaze heavenward
And my soul hitherto bursting with
Its acclaim of wisdom cringes in apprehension
As it beholds the transcend peace above

There are times
When I give up all my chores
To gaze at fellow men
My soul turns feeble with the realization that
I am one lonesome soul

There are times
When troubled and perplexed
I take a walk through dust-filled roads
And lush green forest of shrubs and flowers
But the solemnity of so serene an abode
Quickens my heart with sorrow

God where art thou at such times?
"My God, my God why hast thou forsaken me?"

One Thing You Can't Do

You made my waiting worthwhile
Now my heart you have mended
I yearn for you with all my heart
As an oasis you quenched my thirst
When I remember these things,
I pour out my soul in me

You made my day and brought me joy
I'm beginning to believe
You can do all things
But then I would be wrong
For you can't break a promise
Now that is one thing you can't do
You made up for us
Even when I was in the wrong

I crave for you with all my might
As a cool shower you soothe my nerves
When I remember these things
I pour out my soul in me

At Last

At last! Thou my fairest and dearest
Art back where thou doth belong
With intense beauty and fairness
Yet even more sublime than
My wildest dreams could ever carve,
I see thee even now as I pen down
My emotions on every smooth curve
That my pen carves on paper.
You are fairer than all that's fair

Oh! How my soul strains with strength
To behold the sweet rose nectar
With which God painted thy lips
And those stars which mere fools
Think to be eyes
(It pains me that men be so low in thought)
Those stars would cause
To be eternally locked away with bliss
The love of those whose stares meet thy gaze

Ah I be a fool
Ah I be a lost fool
When I love you with all my heart
But I am not loved in return,
At last! Thou my fairest and dearest
At back where thou doth belong

God's love

Never has such love been ever
Never will this love fail ever
· Although some things seem eternal
Like the deep blue ocean is one
That seems forever to go on
But my love surely last much more daily

The least ways that it grows
Is uncountable immeasurable and infinite
Just as the sun surely rises
And sets at its due time
Every morning and evening time
So is my love forever steadfast

The rich foamy sparkling bubbles
That rides with the ocean waves
The rich brightly colored rainbow
That comes with the sun after the rain
May to the eye seem eternal
Yet my love surpasses all

Giving

There is a place in your heart
That reaches out to the man on the street
There is a place in that heart of yours
That wants to share

Follow your heart and give
So he can have a home
You will find that you have given
To yourself something even greater

There is a place in that smile of yours
That is not completely filled with joy
There is a place on that smooth face of yours
That will do with some more smiles

That place can be filled with giving
That place can be full by sharing
You will find that you have given
To yourself something even much more greater

Hold Fast

Hold fast within thy heart dreams
With realms in spheres light years away
Dream of the battles thou would fight
In the constellation of Orion
Dream of treatise of peace and love
That you will miss due to compromise
When victory alas was so near

Keep your dreams dear to your heart
Make them part of you
And with honor and integrity
Seek out and feed your wildest imaginations
Conquer through friendship
Enemies that you have been taught
To dream to conquer through violence,
Pursue your dreams till they seek
For themselves crevice in the soul of every man
In hope of some fulfillment

Cast away the fantasies
Which have overcome your purity of thought
Dream if of nothing
Of the rising and setting of the sun
And the stars in their vast array
Cast away the dark shadow
Of disappointment and despair

Which thy unfulfilled dreams cast,
Throw some smiles on new dreams
Noble and pure in character
In your dreams
Choose right above wrong
And life on earth will be better
Because of your dreams and choice

I Will Bear Your Name

Holding the pen in my hand today
I run out of words to express my joy
For the love you have showered on me
Ever before I was born
For being here for me
Whenever I needed a friend,
You are always here with me
Everyday and every time
It's time for you to know
Just how I feel with gratitude

So I will bear your name
Where ever I go
I will call your name
Whatever I do
I will seek your face
When ever I wake
Where ever when ever whatever
You are the one for me

All For My Sake

I was sitting alone one lonely afternoon
When I realized that you were beside me
You had your eyes fastened upon me
With an honest smile on your face
And I could not help falling in love with you
I knew you have always being here
Patiently waiting for me
Knowing I will come someday
You never forced yourself on me
Although it was killing you to see me
Throw all that you have given me away
After you gave up all you had for my sake.
Now I yield to you all that I have
Since I now know that your love is true

Sing A Song

Sing a song Bethlehem of a star
That shines in broad daylight
Out shinning the sun even at noon
For unto you today is born a child
That is from the very genesis,
The very genesis of earth's foundation;
Sing a song Bethlehem devoid of melancholy
For Romans stand conquered at His birth
Sing a song Bethlehem of incomprehensible love
For he who is from eternity
Is today a baby upon thy breast

The Light

From way down within
I can see this light shinning through,
It's like seeing land
After being for ever at sea
Like beholding trees on the beach
And seeing fellow human
Whose countenance show
The most elusive peace and joy
Huh! I see land

I always knew I was lost
But I never knew how lost,
My ship was more grandiose than titanic
Bigger than the imagination of folks who sought
To portray beauty in shapes and colors;
Her beauty was so alluring
It kind of made you want to be at sea
Be at sea forever
I thought it was life at its best

I was lost not only at sea
But also on sea
I wondered where I was,
Where I was headed
And where I started out,
So I cried out in misery
For I have lost sight of the sun

And day was no longer different from night

I had become so crippled within myself
That I cried out
And you heard my cry.
You removed the blindfolds from my eyes
Rolled away the dark clouds that blocked the sun
Now I can see your light shine through me
And rejoice in your peaceful light

Life At Its Peak

I sat at life's corridor yesterday
All by myself
When the whirlwind came along
A cute little thing it was while it lasted
Excitement filled the air
The papers jumped and flied
The grasses swayed and danced
And the leaves hopped for a wild ride

Then Billy came to me
As I sat there amazed
Life gradually crept back into my world
Crescendo, accelerando life at its peak
Then they were all gone
Billy and the hopping leaves were all gone
They left me love and joy
They left me an assurance
Can you guess what it was?

Reminiscence

Some time ago
I got to know you real good
And I came to really love and admire you
But I didn't really accept you
You are the very best I've ever known
The closest one to my heart
And the least I can do
Is to make you what else
But the very center of my existence

I know I've said this a million times before
And I've never being good at lying to you,
You are the best I've ever known
The closest one to my heart
And the least I can do
Is to make you what else
But the very center of my existence
I now realize
You are the best there can and will ever be
So here I offer my whole being to you
Renew thy spirit within me

Love Is

All my life I've been lost at sea
Wondering what would make life worthwhile
Heard that life is all about loving and sharing
But I never felt what was meant by care or love
Until you walked right into my life
 And showed me the meaning of love

Love is when you smile at me
Love is when I look in your eyes
Love is when you say I love you
Love is when I feel your touch
Love is when I reach out and you are there
Love is when you gave your life for me

I am not a saint
But I know one when I see one
I am not an angel
But I give my all and all
To have you with me
I just can't thank God enough
For every morn that I wake up
And see the sun rise from the east
And for giving me one more day
Now that I know what love means
Love is you

Consolers' Fallacies

Weep no more dear one
Though he that thou didst love is gone
A strong bulwark he was
When cruel death sort him

Thou surely belie thyself
If thou fails his smile to remember
It was of the order of the pretty stars
When they break through thick clouds at night

Thousands of the rank of Pharaohs
In vain did shoot arrows of envy
Against his pure heart of steel
Indeed, his heart was as the cedar of Lebanon

It's true the number of them
Whose gruesome guffaw at thy loss
Are as the stars in the sky
Fear not, for he shall let their smile remain
Thus far off

Thy heart's brave-heart is gone
He is gone to be closer to thee
So weep no more
Hold him dear still close to thy heart
He though dead shall return thy love

It's Your Day

Your day is here babe and I am thinking
About what you would be doing
Now that you are by yourself
Spending your day alone
Can't help smiling babe
When I remember your broad smile
I thank God for you
And for your life

It's your birthday
How are you doing wherever you are?
Today is the greatest day in my life
For you were born today
Does he even remember that
It's your day?

Has he said happy birthday
Or will he just say 'how do you do' today?
Hope you are very happy?
Everyday as I pray for you
I thank God for you
You are the most beautiful gal
You changed my whole life
Happy birthday babe

Happy birthday babe
Wish you were here
So I could hold you in my arms
And say happy birthday
Right into your ear
Happy birthday babe

God Trust You

Talking about your love
She stands in complete awe
That father of the whole world
Bestow all his love on this his ward

While discussing your grace
With another daughter in this race
How you reveal the future
All of which happen for sure

You opened her eyes to your trust
Do not be distraught
Was the unequivocal admonition
God trust you and needs your cooperation

Treachery In The Air

Woe! Woe!! Woe!!!
Here lay the bodies of our kinfolks
They joyfully set out this morning
Never realizing it's a day of mourning
Oh woe! We wail grievously

Tragedy! Tragedy!! Tragedy!!!
We were in a sleep
When they slipped in
Oh what tragedy
What an ominous tragedy
What a terrible wake up call

Terror! Terror!! Terror!!!
There is treachery in the air
We lift our voices and weep
We weep for our brothers and sisters
We weep for our parents and children
Hijacked unto death and its cold arm

Horror! Horror!! Horror!!!
Oh Horror! We wail and cry
How did we forsake our watch?
How did they forget the touch?
Of the innate ultimate respect of life
Who will replace this irreplaceable lost?
Who will fill this great void born of loss?

Who shall console us?
Who shall comfort us?

None but Jesus can contemplate our tomorrow
None but Jesus can appreciate our sorrow
None but Jesus can alleviate our pain
None but Jesus can experience our distress
None but Jesus understands our plight
None can put us to flight
Jesus is our solace
He will not fail
In him we will prevail

Siblings

Just like siblings
We are of various shapes and shades
We often whine and quarrel
We feel we deserve more and better
We are complete as we compete
We have our rivalry
Just like siblings

Just like siblings
We stand united and form a union
We unite against all that threaten
We surrender not to adversity or the adversary
We succumb not to violence
None can separate or intimidate us
Just like siblings

Just like siblings
We are planted by fathers' discipline and principles
We uphold our mothers' praise and grace
We are one in our pain and gain
We stand decisive and indivisible
We are discrete as we share secrets
We cherish the lyrics of our life
Just like siblings

Just like siblings
We cast aside all fears and cares
And thank God for our freedom
For this nation is built on him,
We will continue to trust in God
By lifting up our heads, hands and hearts
Just like siblings

Just like siblings
We maintain that in God we trust
We remember how he sustains us
We remember how far he has brought us
He is our father and founder
We are his children and kindred
Just like siblings

Epilogue

Oh how joy feels my soul

When thy mercy make manifest in me

Words whose meaning and rhyme

Fill my heart with wonder

It is amazing the power

That overflows my soul

When pretty faces

With love open their mouths

And thy praise utter with candor

So inasmuch as this mortal flesh

Shall from you breath lend

And my lips shall find it possible

Find it possible to utter a word

Thus shall I allow thy mercy make manifest in me

Words whose meanings and rhyme

Fill human breast with wonder

i

Title/First Line	Page

Title/First Line	Page

Title/First Line	Page

Just Like Siblings Order Form

Use this convenient order form to order additional copies
of
Just Like Siblings

Please Print:

Name_____

Address_____

City_____ **State**_____

Zip_____

Phone(**)**_____

_____ copies of book @ $13.95 each $ _____

Postage and handling @ $3.85 per book $ _____

NC residents add 6.5% tax $ _____

Total amount enclosed $ _____

Make checks payable to:

Blessed Oki
13 S. Berrymeadow Lane
Durham, NC 27703